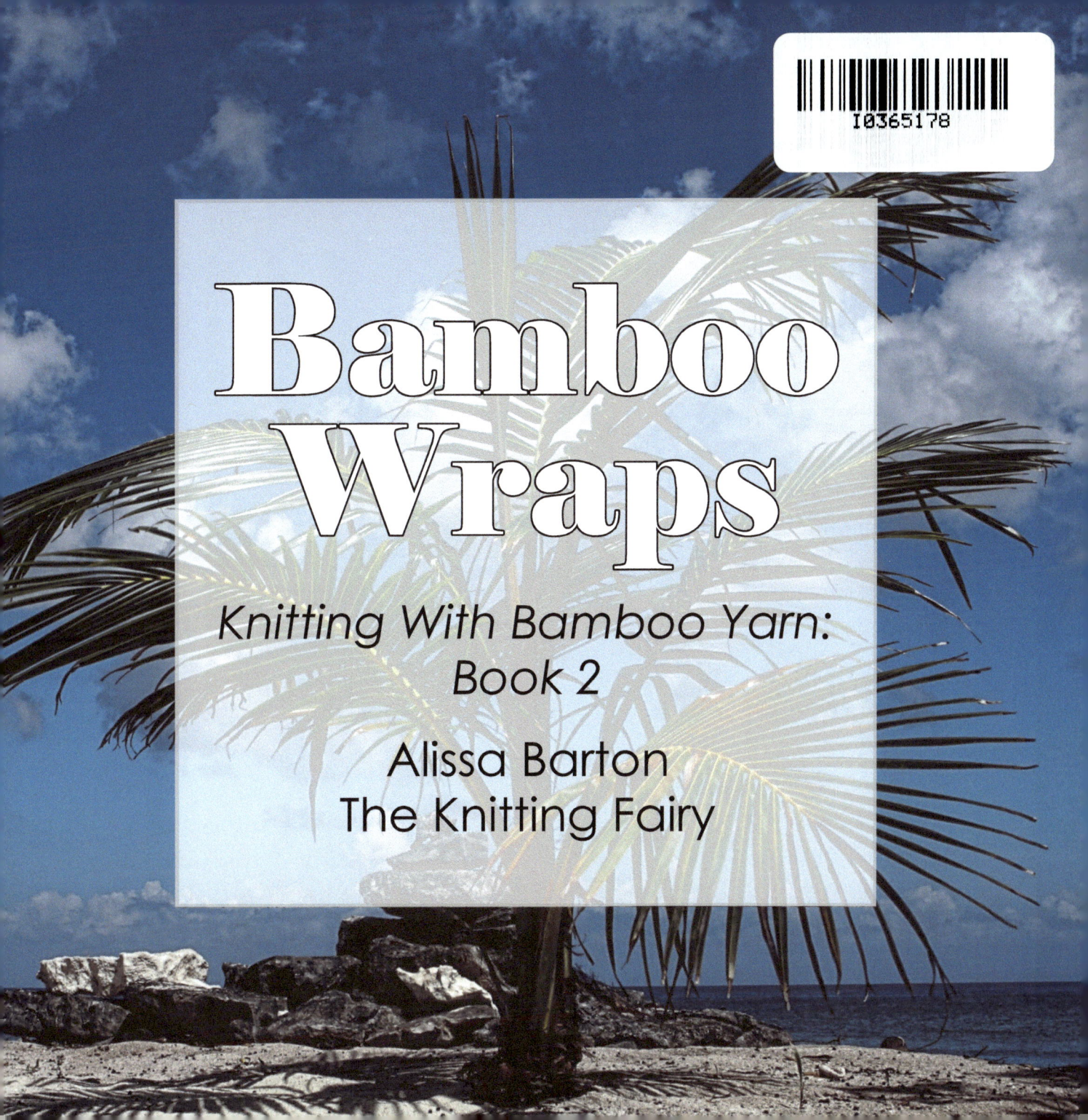

Bamboo Wraps

Knitting With Bamboo Yarn: Book 2

Alissa Barton
The Knitting Fairy

Bamboo Wraps
Knitting With Bamboo Yarn: Book 2
Alissa Barton, The Knitting Fairy

Copyright ©2019 by Alissa Barton
All Rights Reserved
All Text and Photography by Alissa and Brad Barton unless otherwise noted

Published by
Jenies Technologies Incorporated and Alissa Barton
2580 W. Camp Wisdom Ste 100 #247
Grand Prairie, TX 75052

http://KnittingFairy.com
Facebook: http://facebook.com/knittingfairy
Twitter: @knittingfairy
Instagram: @theknittingfairy

First Printing
ISBN: 978-1-7340173-0-4

No part of this book may be reproduced, stored, or transmitted in any form or by any means, electronic, mechanical, photo copied, recorded, or otherwise, without prior express, written consent from the author and publisher.

Knitting Fairy is a trademark of Jenies Technologies Incorporated

Introduction

Bamboo is silky and shiny. It has amazing drape. It's cool to the touch, warm (but not hot) to the skin. It travels well and the list goes on.

What I love the most about bamboo is the way that the colors just seem to glow. In the hands of a master dyer, it takes on a life of it's own. Jennifer at Theodora's Pearls is certainly a master dyer. I couldn't resist the opportunity to take more of her yarn and turn it into things to wrap myself up in. So I created this book: Bamboo Wraps.

All of the wraps in this collection are big. Big enough to wrap around you and chase the chill away or drape with that perfect flair to set off a special outfit. I have chosen models of all sizes so that maybe you can identify how a particular wrap will look on you better. I am grateful to my models, who take the time to come and let me play dress-up on them and who exhibit my creations with such grace and ease. Believe me, you don't want me to have to model them!

Lastly, you can really see how these wraps look through the beauty of my husband's photography. Brad is an award-winning photographer (often taking pictures of things that have NOTHING to do with yarn) and his talents are what make this book take on a life of its own. I am constantly in awe of his talent and thrilled that he is willing to take the time to photograph and edit this book for me.

#knittingfairybamboo

Table of Contents

6. Boho Shrug

10. Striations Shawl

16. Quick How-To on Helix Knitting

20. Whirlpool Poncho

28. Whitecap Beach Wrap

36. Terms and Abbreviations

38. Credits

39. Fairy Facts

#knittingfairybamboo

This easy to knit, easy to wear wrap is suitable for most adult sizes. For reference, I wear a 2X and it fits me comfortably.

Finished size: 16" Deep, 36" Back Shoulder Width

Materials Needed:
Auxanometer by Theodora's Pearls: 1 full skein each of 3 colors (1200 yds total)
US #5 (3.75mm) 32" circular knitting needle
5 Locking stitch markers

Gauge: 6.3 sts and 9.25 rows = 1" in half linen stitch, blocked.

Half Linen stitch pattern:
Row 1: Purl.
Row 2: (RS) (K1, S1pwyf) repeat across to last 2 sts, end K2.
Row 3: Purl.
Row 4: (RS) K1, (K1, S1pwyf) repeat across to last stitch, end K1.

Directions:
With color A, evenly cast on 466 sts. Place a locking stitch marker into the exact middle (after stitch 233) of the cast on edge and leave it there in the cast on for the duration of the knit. You will need this marker for finishing later. This entire piece is worked in the Half Linen stitch pattern as written above. Continue working your 4-row linen stitch repeat while changing colors in the following sequence:

Work half linen stitch using color A for 38 rows. Do not break color A.
Join in color B and (work 2 rows of color B, then 2 rows of color A) five times. (20 rows total) Break Color A.
Work half linen stitch using color B for 38 rows. Do not break color B.
Join in color C and (work 2 rows of color C, then 2 rows of color B) five times. (20 rows total). Break color B.
Work half linen stitch using color C for 38 rows.
Bind off in color C using this method: Knit the first 2 stitches one at a time. **2 stitches now on right needle. Reinsert the tip of the left needle through both stitches from left to right and out the front. Wrap the working yarn around the right (back) needle and k2togtbl. This leaves one stitch on your right hand needle. Knit the next stitch normally. Repeat from ** until all stitches have been worked and only a single stitch remains on the right hand needle. Break MC and feed through last stitch. Pull tight.

Block flat to 74" long, 16" wide. Leave the marker in the center of the cast on in place. While it is pinned out, before you remove any pins- place one stitch marker 2" to the right of the center marker and another 2" to the left of the center marker, and then a second set another 16" from those.

When you have removed it from the blocking mats, orient it with the right side facing down. Bring the short ends of the rectangle up to match the stitch markers you placed along the cast on edge and sew the short ends to the cast on edge to form the shoulders and sleeves starting at the marker you placed 2" from center, ending at the outer most markers.

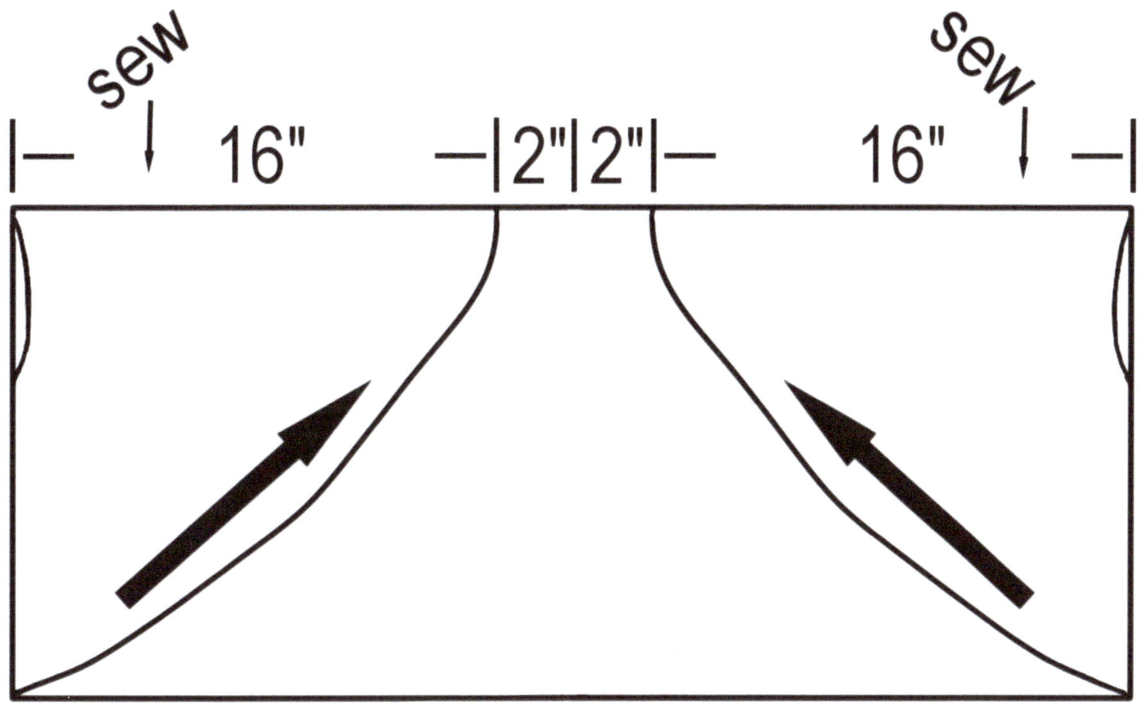

sew ↓ |— 16" —| |—2"|2"|— |— 16" ↓ sew —|

Striations Shawl

Finished Size: 70" long, 23" deep

Materials Needed:
3 skeins 100 grams Auxanometer,
100% bamboo fingering weight by Theodora's Pearls. Shown in A) Rust, B) Sand Dune, C) Sage grotto
US #6, 32" circ

Gauge: 5.3 Sts = 1" on US #6 in center lace pattern, blocked

Directions:
With Color C, loosely cast on 119 sts.
Row 1: S1pwyf, K118.
Row 2: S1pwyf, K9, K2tog, (K5, YO, K1, YO, K5, S1K2togPsso) 6 times, K5, YO, K1, YO, K5, SSK, K10.
Row 3: S1pwyf, K118.
Repeat rows 2 & 3 three times more, DO NOT BREAK C, carry unused color up the side throughout this stripe sequence LOOSELY.
With Color A, work rows 2 & 3 once. DO NOT BREAK A.
With Color C, work rows 2 & 3 three times. DO NOT BREAK C.
With Color A, work rows 2 & 3 twice. DO NOT BREAK A.
With Color C, work rows 2 & 3 twice. DO NOT BREAK C.
WIth Color A, work rows 2 & 3 three times. DO NOT BREAK A.
With Color C, work rows 2 & 3 once. Break color C.
Bottom garter border is complete.
Begin stockinette section continuing with only color A.

Row 1: S1pwyf, K9, K2tog, (K5, YO, K1, YO, K5, S1K2togPsso) 6 times, K5, YO, K1, YO, K5, SSK, K10.

Row 2: S1pwyf, K9, P to last 10 sts, K10.

Repeat these two rows with color A only until the section measures 16" (approx 120 rows) OR 30 yards of color A remains.

Transition stripes, add in color B continue the stockinette section as established, striping in the following sequence. DO NOT BREAK colors between stripes, carry the unused color loosely up the side.

Work
- 2 rows color B
- 6 rows color A
- 4 rows color B
- 4 rows color A
- 6 rows color B
- 2 rows color A. Break color A.

Work second solid section the same as the first solid section using only color B until the second solid section measures 16" (approx 120 rows) or until 30 yards of color B remain.

Transition stripes, add in color C. Continue the stockinette section as established, striping in the following sequence. DO NOT BREAK colors between stripes, carry the unused color loosely up the side.

Work
- 2 rows color C
- 6 rows color B
- 4 rows color C
- 4 rows color B
- 6 rows color C
- 2 rows color B. Break color B.

Work third solid section the same as the first solid section using color C only until the second solid section measures 16" (approx 120 rows) or until 30 yards of color C remain.
Garter border stripes, add in color A.
Work ending section in garter stitch. DO NOT BREAK colors between stripes, carry the unused color loosely up the side.

With color A:
Row 1: S1pwyf, K9, K2tog, (K5, YO, K1, YO, K5, S1K2togPsso) 6 times, K5, YO, K1, YO, K5, SSK, K10.
Row 2: S1pwyf, K118.
Repeating these last two rows, work in the following color sequence:
      6 rows color C
      4 rows color A
      4 rows color C
      6 rows color A
      2 rows color C,
          break color C.
      8 rows A.
Bind off in pattern using color A
Weave in ends, block to size.

A Quick How-To on Helix Knitting

The Whirlpool Poncho employs a fabulous technique for getting jog-less color stripes called Helix Knitting. Essentially, when you are knitting one thread in the round you are making a single "Helix" or spiral. The yarn goes round and round, endlessly forming one layer upon another - exactly like those Slinkys we used to play with as children. Did you ever get a second Slinky and get it tangled into the first? If you took those two and just slide them together you end up with two spirals, running round and round together. Imagine if you took 6 or 7 or 14 and nestled them together... they would all continue around in their spiral but each is slightly further apart than it would be on it's own. That is Helix knitting. Several spirals all running around the circle at the same time but minding their own business. It sounds complicated, but really all you are doing is knitting. We can knit! The number of strands will determine the angle of the spiral, more strands, the more steep the spiral. Whirlpool uses 14 strands, each running its own race around the work. I wanted spirals of varying thickness, so there are more spirals of some colors, side by side, to create a thicker looking spiral. If you would like to give it a try without 14 strands, grab some extra yarn and needles and try this with me. I have worsted weight and size 8 16" circs in the photos.

Begin by casting on 20 sts of each color onto your needle. I did not join the sections of colors, just cast them on, one after another. There are 80 sts on my needle.

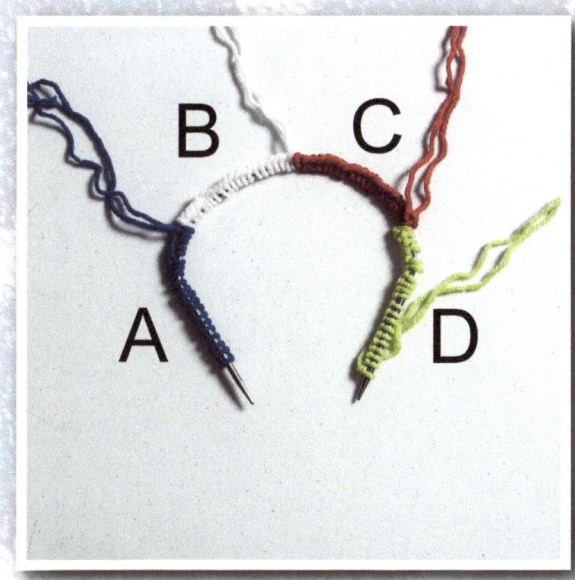

You can place a marker onto the right needle tip at the end of section D. This will help you keep up with the beginning of the round.

Pick up color D and carry it across the gap between D and A. Knit color D over all of the stitches in the color A section. It looks like color A has disappeared, just wait.

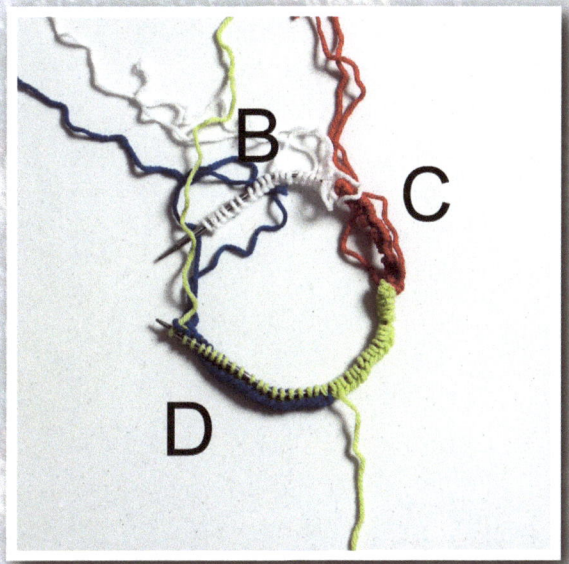

Leave color D there and pick up color A to the left of color D, without twisting the two together. Knit color A across the stitches in color B. Now it looks like color B is gone. Wait for it...

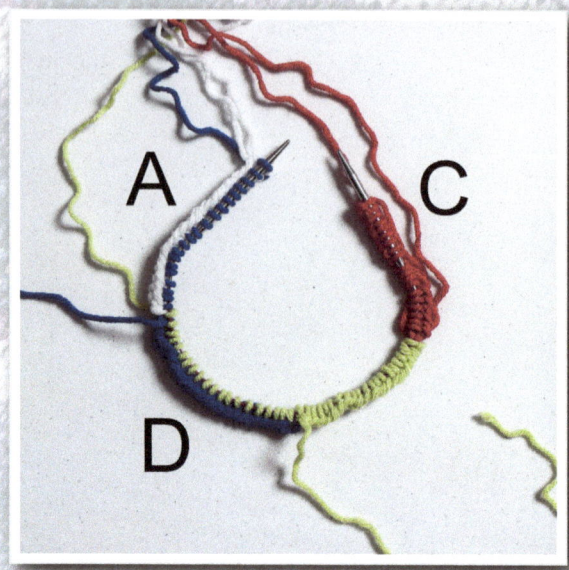

Leave color A there and pick up color B to the left of color A, without twisting the two together. Knit color B across the stitches in color C.

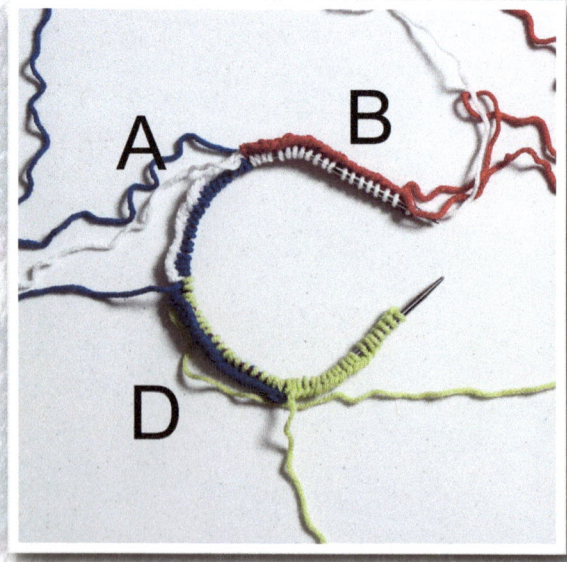

Leave color B there and pick up C to the left of color B, without twisting the two together. Knit color C across the stitches in color D.

You can see that each color section has rotated one quarter of the way around the circle. We have knitted 4 separate quarters of one round.

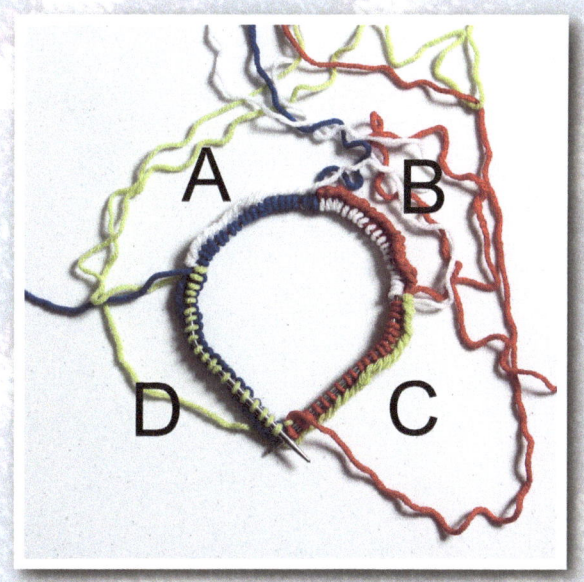

When you have complete one round with color D you have actually created 4 rounds. This set of 4 rounds is called a course.

The yarn will wrap itself together as you knit, creating a very bright umbilical of yarn. Do not fret! If you leave the balls of yarn in the same position while you work they are not tangled. Just pick up your knitting and rotate it in the opposite direction to untwist the umbilical and they will all go right back into place. You can untwist as often as you want. I usually only do it when it annoys me or I am getting ready to put it away for the time being.

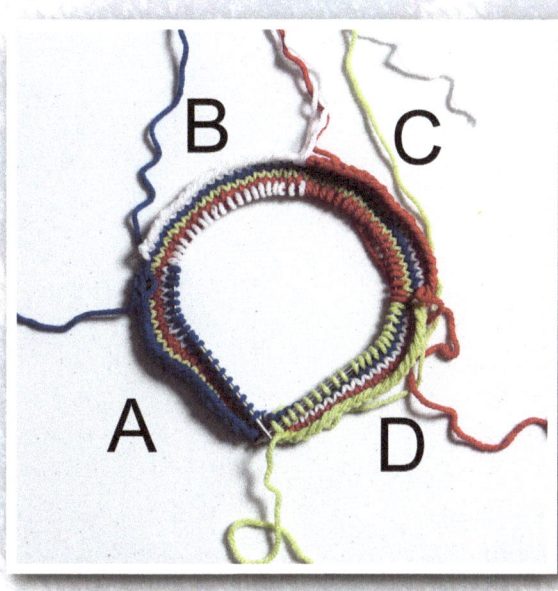

Whirlpool Poncho

Finished Size: 18" from front neck to bottom hem

Materials Needed:
Auxanometer, 100% bamboo fingering weight by Theodora's Pearls. Shown in A) Blueberry- 2 skeins,
B) Hydrangea - 1 skein, C) Alabaster - 1skein,
D) Fuchsia Passion -50g, 1 mini skein.
US #6, 24" and 32"circ
US #2 16" circ
13 Removable stitch markers
1 different marker for beginning of round

Gauge: 5.5 Sts = 1" on US #6 in stockinette stitch, blocked

Directions:
With color A and 24" #6 circ, loosely cast on 131 sts. Join to work in rounds. Place a marker for beginning of round.

Rnd 1: (K1, P1) repeat to last stitch, end K1.
Rnd 2: (P1, K1) repeat to last stitch, end P1.
Repeat rnds 1&2 for 6".

Change to US#2 16".
Knit 3 rnds.

Change to US#6 24" circ.
Begin working short row section, also in color A.
Rnd 1: Knit.
Rnd 2: (short rows) K 65, W&T.
P65, W&T.
K 75 (knitting the wrap and stitch together when you come to it), W&T.
P85 (purling the wrap and stitch together when you come to it), W&T.
K95 (knitting the wrap and stitch together when you come to it), W&T.
P105 (purling the wrap and stitch together when you come to it), W&T.
K115 (knitting the wrap and stitch together when you come to it), W&T.
P125 (purling the wrap and stitch together when you come to it), W&T.
K30.
Rnd 3: Knit around, working the last two wrapped stitches together with their wraps as you come to them.
Rnd 4: (K15, Kfb) 8 times, Knit to last st of Rnd, KFb. (140 sts)

Begin Working Helix Pattern:
Wind each of your colors into 25g balls. Color A: 6 balls, color B: 4 balls, color C: 3 balls, color D: 1 ball. You will have some of Color A left. You can wind it and set it aside for the bottom hem. Each ball will become one helix stripe. Set up as follows: K10 with the first ball of color A, (pm), [join the next ball of color A, K10, (pm)] 5 times, [join the next ball of color B, K10, (pm)] 4 times, [join the next ball of color C, K10, (pm)] 3 times, join the ball of color D, K10. You are at the beginning of round and all 14 balls of yarn are attached. You are now working 14 rounds simultaneously. Each "course" through the colors will result in one set of 14 "rounds". It is imperative that you do not twist any of the yarns as you knit through the rounds. As you come to each stitch marker you will drop the previous ball to the right and pick up the next from the left.

Course 1:
Rnd 1: (K1, Kfb) five times in color D (m), [K10 in color A, (m)] 6 times, [K10 in color B, (m)] 4 times, [K10 in color C, (m)] 3 times. 145 sts.
Rnd 2: [K15 in color C, (m)], [(K1, Kfb) five times in color D], [K10 in color A, (m)] 6 times, [K10 in color B, (m)] 4 times, [K10 in color C, (m)] twice. 150 sts.
Rnd 3: [K15 in color C, (m)] twice, [(K1, Kfb) five times in color D], [K10 in color A, (m)] 6 times, [K10 in color B, (m)] 4 times, [K10 in color C, (m)]. 155 sts.
Rnd 4: [K15 in color C, (m)] 3 times, [(K1, Kfb) five times in color D], [K10 in color A, (m)] 6 times, [K10 in color B, (m)] 4 times. 160 sts.
Rnd 5: [K15 in color B, (m)], [K15 in color C, (m)] 3 times, [(K1, Kfb) five times in color D], [K10 in color A, (m)] 6 times, [K10 in color B, (m)] 3 times. 165 sts.

Rnd 6: [K15 in color B, (m)] twice, [K15 in color C, (m)] 3 times, [(K1, Kfb) five times in color D], [K10 in color A, (m)] 6 times, [K10 in color B, (m)] twice. 170 sts.

Rnd 7: [K15 in color B, (m)] 3 times, [K15 in color C, (m)] 3 times, [(K1, Kfb) five times in color D], [K10 in color A, (m)] 6 times, [K10 in color B, (m)]. 175 sts.

Rnd 8: [K15 in color B, (m)] 4 times, [K15 in color C, (m)] 3 times, [(K1, Kfb) five times in color D], [K10 in color A, (m)] 6 times. 180 sts.

Rnd 9: [K15 in color A, (m)], [K15 in color B, (m)] 4 times, [K15 in color C, (m)] 3 times, [(K1, Kfb) five times in color D], [K10 in color A, (m)] 5 times. 185 sts.

Rnd 10: [K15 in color A, (m)] twice, [K15 in color B, (m)] 4 times, [K15 in color C, (m)] 3 times, [(K1, Kfb) five times in color D], [K10 in color A, (m)] 4 times. 190 sts.

Rnd 11: [K15 in color A, (m)] 3 times, [K15 in color B, (m)] 4 times, [K15 in color C, (m)] 3 times, [(K1, Kfb) five times in color D], [K10 in color A, (m)] 3 times. 195 sts.

Rnd 12: [K15 in color A, (m)] 4 times, [K15 in color B, (m)] 4 times, [K15 in color C, (m)] 3 times, [(K1, Kfb) five times in color D], [K10 in color A, (m)] twice. 200 sts.

Rnd 13: [K15 in color A, (m)] 5 times, [K15 in color B, (m)] 4 times, [K15 in color C, (m)] 3 times, [(K1, Kfb) five times in color D], [K10 in color A, (m)]. 205 sts.

Rnd 14: [K15 in color A, (m)] 6 times, [K15 in color B, (m)] 4 times, [K15 in color C, (m)] 3 times, [(K1, Kfb) five times in color D]. 210 sts.

This completes course #1. You will now continue in the same fashion, but with 15 stitches in each section and each time you work the section in color D you will use the following increase pattern instead:

Course 2: [(K2, Kfb) five times in color D] (adds 5 stitches each time, 70 stitches in the entire course), end with 20 sts in each section. 280 sts total.

Course 3: [(K3, Kfb) five times in color D] (adds 5 stitches each time, 70 stitches in the entire course), end with 25 sts in each section. 350 sts total.

Course 4: [(K4, Kfb) five times in color D] (adds 5 stitches each time, 70 stitches in the entire course), end with 30 sts in each section. 420 sts total.

Course 5: [(K5, Kfb) five times in color D] (adds 5 stitches each time, 70 stitches in the entire course), end with 35 sts in each section. 490 sts total.

Course 6: [(K6, Kfb) five times in color D] (adds 5 stitches each time, 70 stitches in the entire course), end with 40 sts in each section. 560 sts total.

Course 7: [(K7, Kfb) five times in color D] (adds 5 stitches each time, 70 stitches in the entire course), end with 45 sts in each section. 630 sts total.

Course 8: [(K8, Kfb) five times in color D] (adds 5 stitches each time, 70 stitches in the entire course), end with 50 sts in each section. 700 sts total.

Break all 14 strands of yarn, leaving 6" tails, remove all markers except the bor marker. Join in your leftover ball of color A.
Hem:
The hem is worked in seed stitch.
I did not work a plain round before beginning my seed stitch hem, but my test knitter did not like the color blips and suggested I add that option. SO, if you do not like color blips, feel free to add one knit round in color A before beginning the seed stitch hem.
Rnd 1: (K1, P1) around to 2 stitches before the bor marker. Kfb, K1. (701 sts)
Rnd 2: (P1, K1) around to the last stitch, end P1.
Rnd 3: (K1, P1) around to the last stitch, end K1.
Rnd 4: (P1, K1) around to the last stitch, end P1.
Bind off loosely in pattern. Weave in ends.

Finished Size: One Size, See Diagram

Materials Needed:
MC - 150g Fingering weight yarn (shown in Auxanometer by Theodora's Pearls, colorway "Cream" 400 yds/115g)
And 6, 50g mini skeins Auxanometer colorways "Little Red Corvette", "Goldenrod", "Blue Sky", "Poppy", "Marigold", "Iced Berry"
US #5 (3.75mm), 32" circular needle
Stitch markers, if desired

Gauge: 4.9 sts and 7.7 rows = 1" in Back Lace. For swatch, cast on 49 sts and work 4 repeats of center repeat on chart A, adding one knit stitch after the final repeat. Block your swatch!

Markers on This Pattern: Use a locking stitch marker and physically PIN it into this stitch. You may move them closer to your needles as the knitting progresses if necessary to keep the marker visible.

Start by Working the Back Lace Panel:
With US #5 circ and (MC) Cream, loosely cast on 101 sts. Work Chart A, rows 1-48 ONCE, working the area between the red lines 6 times. Do not miss those single stockinette stitches on the far right and left of the chart. You will need these later for picking up stitches in the wings.
Work Chart B, rows 1-48 ONCE, working the area between the red lines 4 times, keeping the first and last stitches in stockinette.
Work Chart C (same as B), rows 1-48 ONCE, working the area between the red lines twice, keeping the first and last stitches in stockinette.
Work Chart D, rows 1-52 ONCE, keeping the first and last stitches in stockinette. Bind off after row 52 and break the yarn.

Back Lace Panel, Chart A

Repeat area between red lines 6 times. Note single stockinette stitch at beginning and end of chart. (Chart Key on page 33.)

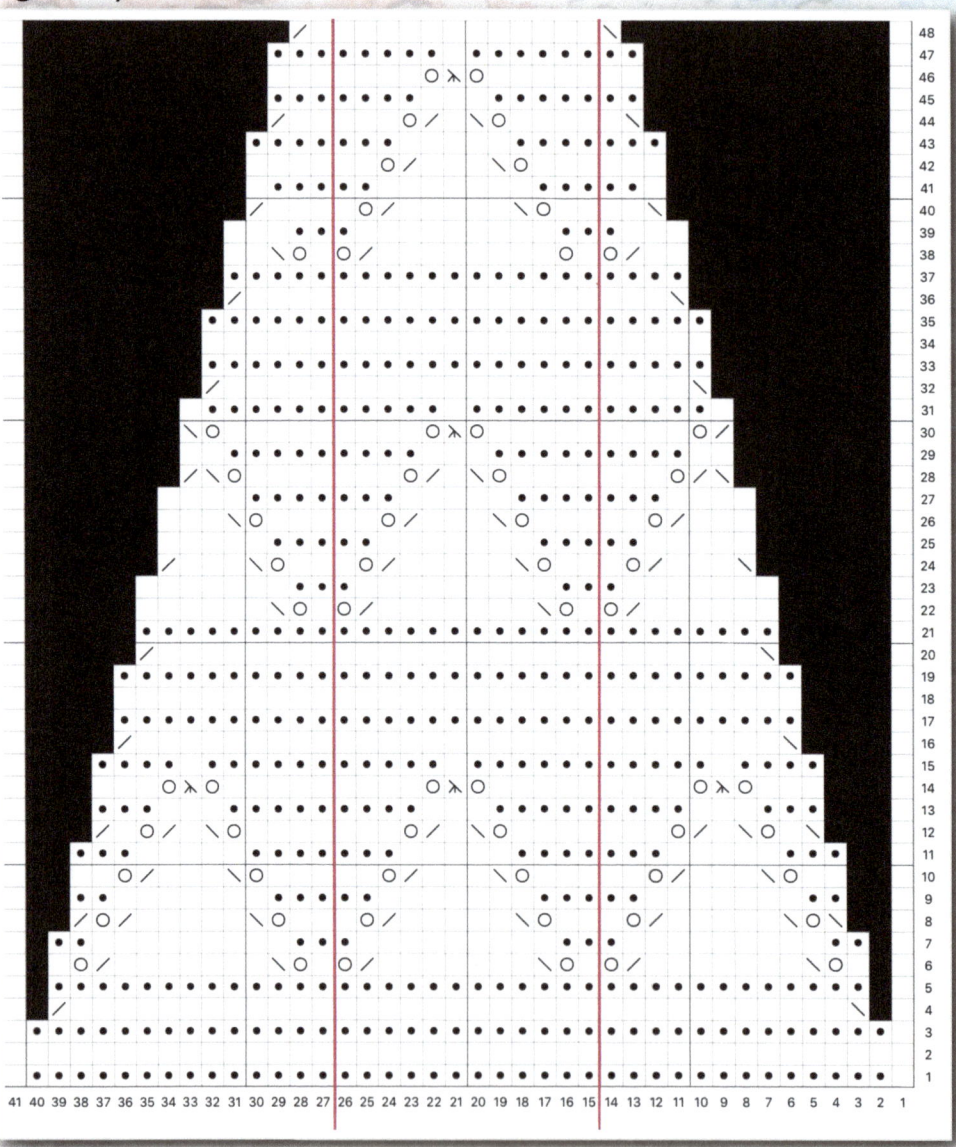

Back Lace Panel, Chart B and C.
For B, work area between red lines 4 times. (Rows 49-96) For C, work area between red lines twice. (Second repeat of rows 49-96) Note single stockinette stitch at beginning and end of chart. (Chart Key on page 33.)

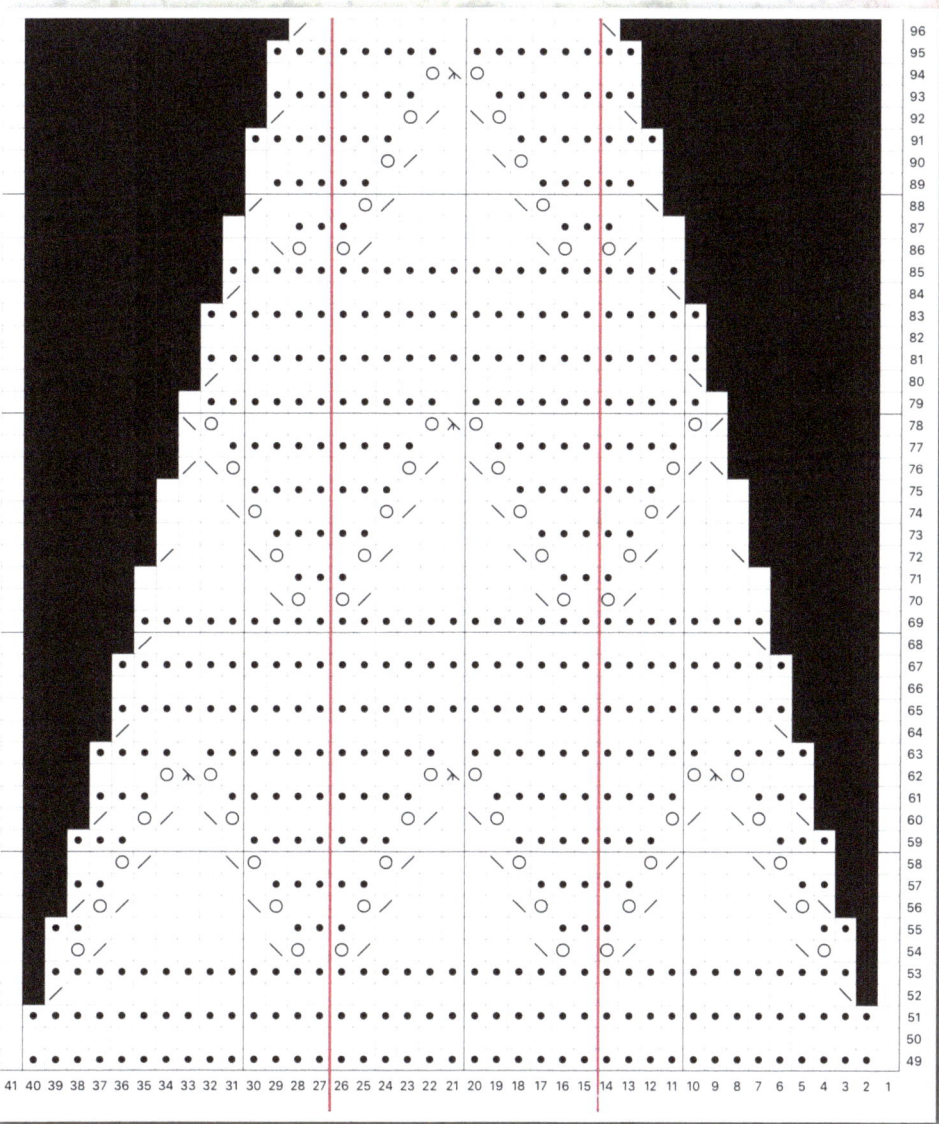

Back Lace Panel, Chart D. Note single stockinette stitch at beginning and end of chart. (Chart Key on page 33.)

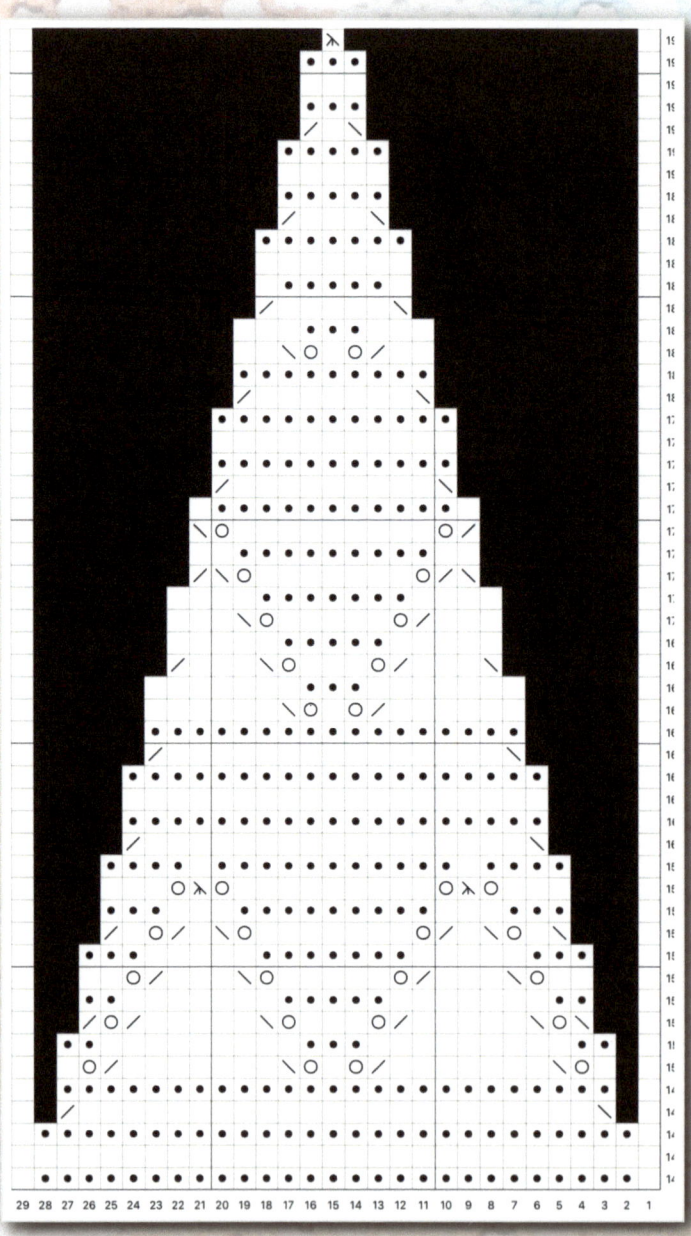

Symbol	Right Side	Wrong Side
□	**k** knit	**p** purl
●	**p** purl	**k** knit
/	**k2tog** knit 2 together	**p2tog** purl 2 together
\	**ssk** slip, slip, knit	**ssp** slip, slip, purl
⋏	**sk2p** sl1, k2tog, psso	**sp2p** sl1 wyif, p2tog tbl, psso
○	**yo** yarn over	**yo** yarn over

Right Wing: With the right side of the triangle facing you and the cast on edge at the bottom, start at the right hand bottom corner, Pick up and knit 132 sts in (MC) Cream.
Rows 1-5: Knit.
Change to (CC)"Little Red Corvette", break (MC).
Row 6: K3, (SSK, YO) across to last 3 sts, K3.
Row 7: Knit.
Repeat rows 6 and 7 9 times more.
Change to (MC) Cream, Break CC.
Row 26: K3, SSK, K to last 3 sts, M1L, K3.
Row 27: Knit.
Repeat rows 26 and 27 twice more.
Break (MC), repeat rows 6-31 once each, changing the CC in the following order: Goldenrod, Blue Sky, Poppy, Marigold, Iced Berry.
Bind off evenly using MC. Do not bind off tightly, but you do not want it ridiculously loose either, the bind off edge needs to block to 24".

Left Wing: With the right side of the triangle facing you, start at the top of the triangle, pick up and knit 132 sts in (MC) Cream.
Rows 1-5: Knit.
Change to (CC) "Little Red Corvette", break (MC).
Row 6: K3, (YO, K2tog) across to last 3 sts, K3.
Row 7: Knit.
Repeat rows 6 and 7 9 times more.
Change to (MC) Cream, Break CC.
Row 26: K3, M1R, K to last 5 sts, K2tog, K3.
Row 27: Knit.
Repeat rows 26 and 27 twice more.
Break (MC), repeat rows 6-31 five times more, changing the CC in the following order: Goldenrod, Blue Sky, Poppy, Marigold, Iced Berry.
Bind off with same tension as right wing using MC.

Block following the measurements on the diagram on page 34.

Terms and Abbreviations

K1 = Knit.

P1 = Purl.

S1(2, 3)pwyb = Slip the indicated number of stitches purlwise with the yarn held in back.

S1Pwyf = slip the next stitch as if to purl with the yarn held in the front.

K2tog = Knit the next 2 stitches together. (1 stitch decreased)

K2togtbl: Knit 2 together through the back loops. (1 stitch decreased)

SK2P = Slip the first stitch as if to knit to the right hand needle, knit the next 2 stitches together, pass the slipped stitch over the decrease. (2 sts decreased)

SSK = Slip one as if to knit, Slip a second stitch as if to knit, insert the left needle tip back into the front of these two stitches (together), wrap the yarn around the right needle and knit these two stitches together through the back loops. (1 stitch decreased)

S1K2togPsso = Slip on stitch as if to knit, Knit the next two stitches together, pass the slipped stitch over. (2 stitches decreased)

Kfb = Knit into the front and the back of this stitch. (1 stitch increased)

(RS) = Right side.

(WS) = Wrong side.

BOR = Beginning of round.

[M] = Marker.

YO = Yarn Over.

BO = Bind off

M1R = Make one stitch, right leaning.

M1L = Make one stitch, left leaning.

(MC) = Main Color.

(CC) = Contrast Color.

(pm) = place marker

W&T = wrap and turn. Move the yarn to the front of the work between the needle tips, slip 1 stitch purlwise, move the yarn to the back of the work, slip the stitch back to the left needle. Turn the work so that you can now work across the same stitches you just worked. As you come to previously wrapped stitches, work the stitch and the wrap together. For the best appearance, make sure the wrap is hidden on the wrong side of the work. On the knit side, slip your right needle tip under the wrap and then into the stitch. On the purl side, slip your right needle tip under the wrap on the back side and then into the stitch as if to purl. Work the two strands together.

Theodora's Pearls yarns are available in fine yarn shops nation-wide. For stockists or to become one contact theodoraspearls.com

Photography by Brad Barton http://bradbarton.us
Follow Brad on Twitter and Instagram @txheadshots

Models:
    Randee Nicole - Boho Shrug and Whirlpool Poncho
        Instagram @kit10queen

    Erin Crawford - Whitecap Beach Wrap
        http://erincrawford.actor

    Lena Morris - Striations Shawl

Test Knitters and Proofreaders:
    Marla Morris
    Lori Sheffield

#knittingfairybamboo

Alissa Barton
Knitting Fairy Original Designs

Throughout her over 45 years as a knitter, Alissa has become addicted to yarn and all the marvelous things that can be done with it. From learning to knit her own creations because there were no patterns that did what she wanted them to do, to owning a yarn shop, and now traveling and teaching knitting Alissa finds she just can't get enough of this "Thing with String". Exploring knitting with bamboo just seems to go hand in hand with the hot Texas climate and so here Alissa is offering her second book in Knitting with Bamboo Yarn. This one is a focus on wraps.

You can follow Alissa's yarn adventures on Facebook, Instagram, and Twitter. You can also bring Alissa to you!

Web: KnittingFairy.com
Facebook: KnittingFairy
Ravelry: KnittingFairy
Twitter: @knittingfairy
Instagram: @theknittingfairy

For teaching and workshop scheduling:
817-247-9210

www.ingramcontent.com/pod-product-compliance
Lightning Source LLC
Chambersburg PA
CBHW041118070526
44584CB00002B/204